SINGING NEWS

TOP 10 SOUTHERN GOSPEL SONGS OF 2007

BRENTWOOD-BENSON® music publishing in association with SINGING NEWS

CONTENTS

Truth Is Marching On

Words and Music by
BARRY WEEKS, TONY WOOD
and JIM BRADY

Slowly ♩ = 67

Gm
3fr.
E♭
Some say that He was just a good man; And
Cm
3fr.
Fsus4
F
e - ven though He died, He was - n't real - ly raised.
Cm7
3fr.
B♭/D
E♭
F
Skep - tics rise and speak their lies.
C
C/E
F
Truth is march - ing on.

Dm7
G
Truth is march - ing on.
Down the
C/E
F
C/G
Fm/A♭
cor - ri - dors of time,
in - vin - ci - ble, di - vine,
un - til
Dm
F
G9sus4
3fr.
all that's false is fi - n'lly gone,
truth is march - ing
F
C
2nd time to Coda
Am
Em/G
D/F♯
on.
2. There will

Gm
3fr.
E♭
25
al - ways be cyn - ics and scoff - ers.
Cm7
3fr.
D
27
Faith has al - ways had its nois - y en - e - mies.
They will
Gm
3fr.
E♭maj7
29
rise up, but on - ly for a mo - ment.
'Cause
Cm7
3fr.
Fsus4
F
31
we see ev - i - dence through the cen - tu - ries:

C m7
3fr.
B♭/D
E♭
F
D.S. al Coda
33
Je - sus Christ,
the Way,
the Life.
CODA
C
35
3
Glo - ry, glo - ry, Hal - le - lu - jah. Glo -
F
D m7
C
37
- ry, glo - ry, Hal - le - lu - jah,
G/B
A m
C/G
D m
G 9sus4
3fr.
39
Glo - ry, glo - ry, Hal - le - lu - jah, His truth is march - ing

D♭ D♭/F G♭ E♭m
42
on. Truth is march - ing on. Truth is march - ing on.
A♭ 4fr. D♭/F G♭
45
Down the cor - ri - dors of time, in -
D♭/A♭ G♭m/A E♭m7
47
vin - ci - ble, di - vine, un - til all that's false is fin - 'lly
G♭ A♭9sus4 4fr. G♭m/A C♭2/G♭ G♭m/E♭ D♭
49
gone, truth is march - ing on.

Strike Up the Band

Words and Music by
DIANNE WILKINSON

Lively, with a bounce ♩ = 97

F
9
planned, pre - pared for those who come by way of Cal - v'ry. It's a
G
C
11
song that the an - gels can - not sing. The re - deemed
F
13
of all the a - ges will be there to sing a - long on a
B♭
15
brand new song nev - er heard by mor - tal man. Oh, I'm

B dim7
F/C
D
17
long - ing for the day when we hear King Je - sus say, "Wel - come to
G7
C
F
19
the Prom - ised Land, strike up the band."
1. We are
2. I can
B♭9
21
liv - ing near the Book of Rev - e - la - tion. From the
just im - ag - ine Da - vid as he's play - ing some sweet
F
23
things we see, we know the time is near. Soon the
song a - bout the Ris - en Ho - ly One. We will

B♭9
25
trum - pet blast will start the cel - e - bra - tion. We will
make the heav - ens ring with hap - py prais - es to God the
G
27
1. C B♭/D D♯dim7 C/E
hear the shout from heav - en, loud and clear. Strike up the band,
Fa - ther, God the Spir - it, God the
2. C B♭/D D♯dim7 C/E C D♭
29
Son, God the Son. Strike up the band,
G♭
31
that an - gel band, as - sem - bled now and read - y to pro -

D7 D♭7 G♭
33
claim heav - en's prais - es to the King; That mu - sic's
35
planned, pre - pared for those who come by way of Cal - v'ry. It's a
A♭7 4fr. D♭
37
song that the an - gels can - not sing. The re - deemed
G♭
39
of all the a - ges will be there to sing a - long on a

C♭
41
brand new song nev - er heard by mor - tal man.
Yes, I'm
C dim7
G♭/D♭
E♭
43
long - ing for the day when we hear King Je - sus say, "Wel - come to
A♭7
4fr.
D♭
G♭
45
the Prom - ised Land, strike up the band."
Oh, I'm
C♭
C dim7
G♭/D♭
47
long - ing for the day when we hear King Je - sus

E♭
A♭7
4fr.
49
say: "Wel - come to the prom - ised
D♭
G♭
C♭7
51
Land. Strike up the band. Strike up the band.
G♭
C♭7
G♭
C♭7
53
Strike up the band. Strike up the band!"
G♭
55

He Will Hide Me

Words and Music by
KYLA ROWLAND

C D G G/B
13
Da - vid, cry - ing, "Mer - cy, Lord, on me." I am E -
C Dsus4 G
17
li - jah in a cave, dread - ing the light of day. I am
A A7 Dsus4 D
21
Dan - iel, hum - bly bowed faith - ful - ly. I am
G C/G G
25
Paul in a pris - on, lift - ing praise to heav - en. I am

G Dm7 G7/B C
29
John cast out but not down. I am
C C♯dim7 3fr. G/D B7 Em C
33
Mo - ses seek - ing shel - ter in the cleft of the rock. Here I
G/D D7 G D/F♯ Em
37
am, Lord; Hide me a - gain. I
D C/D G Em
41
fin - al - ly made it to the cleft of the rock. I'm

D C/D D G G/B
glad for I could no long - er stand. Man - y
C C♯dim7 3fr. G/D B/D♯ Em C
times I will strug - gle to reach that old rock, but He will
G/D D7 G/B B aug
hide me a - gain and a - gain.
C C/D D♭/E♭ A♭ 4fr. D♭/A
2. Now, I'm safe from the stran - ger,

A♭
4fr.
A♭/C
4fr.
D♭
E♭
61
safe from the dan - ger that would try to do me great
A♭
4fr.
D♭
E♭
65
harm. I am wrapped up and warm in the
A♭
4fr.
B♭7
69
love of my Mas - ter. I am rest - ing while I lean on His
E♭sus4
E♭7
A♭
4fr.
D♭/A♭
73
arm. So I'll stay a lit - tle long - er un -

A♭ A♭ E♭m A♭/C
77
til I am strong - er when all of my heal - ing is
D♭ D♭ D dim7
81
done. The rav - ens will feed me, and
A♭/E♭ C F m D♭ A♭/E♭ E♭ D♭/E♭ E♭
85
His hand will keep me and hide me 'til I can go
A♭ E♭/G F m E♭ D♭/E♭
89
on. I fin - al - ly made it to the

A♭
4fr.
B♭7/D
E♭
D♭/E♭
E♭
93
cleft of the rock. I'm glad for I could no long - er
A♭
4fr.
D♭
D dim7
97
stand. Man - y times I will strug - gle to
A♭/E♭
4fr.
C7/E
Fm
D♭
A♭/E♭
4fr.
E♭
101
reach that old rock, but He will hide me a - gain and a -
A♭
4fr.
B♭7/F
E♭
E♭/D♭
105
gain. He hid - eth my soul in the

A♭/C D♭ A♭ B♭m D♭/E♭ C m/E♭ B♭m/D♭
4fr. 4fr. 3fr.
109
cleft of the rock that shad - ows a dry, thirst - y
A♭/C E sus4 A/C♯ C♯aug
4fr.
113
land. He hid - eth my life with the
D D♯dim7 A/E E D/E E
117
depths of His love, and He will hide me a - gain and a -
N.C. C 6 B♭maj7 A
121
gain.

My Anchor of Hope

Words and Music by
RODNEY GRIFFIN

G
F/C
13
with - out an an - chor. There was no hope for
C
Em7(♭5)
F
16
me. For - ev - er drift - ing,
C
D7
G7
19
for - ev - er lost till I knew hope was
Dm7
Em/G
G7
C
B♭/D
C7/E
22
of - fered on an old rug - ged cross. I cast my

F
C
an - chor of hope in - to the sea of
D m/C
C
grace. I am moved by sin's wa - ters no
G sus4
G
C/E
F
more. And I'll keep trust - ing in
C
F
Him un - til I see His face. For

C/G
G7
C
C/E
He is my an - chor of hope.
F
C/G
G7
Yes, Je - sus is my an - chor of
C
F♭maj7
hope.
E♭m7
D♭

D♭
49
2. With - out my an - chor, I'm like all the
E♭/B♭
A♭
4fr.
52
rest, a - drift on the wa - ter, a
G♭/D♭
D♭
Fm7(♭5)
G♭
55
fail - ure at best. But since I
D♭/F
A♭7/E♭
4fr.
D♭
E♭7/B♭
58
trust - ed in His pow - er to save, the

A♭ 4fr.
E♭m7 Fm/A♭ A♭7 4fr.
61
winds may be blow - ing, but I'm here to
D♭ E♭m D♭7/F G♭
64
stay. I cast my an - chor of hope in - to the
D♭ D♭/A♭ D♭
67
sea of grace. I am moved by sin's
A♭sus4 4fr. A♭ 4fr. D♭/F
70
wa - ters no more. I'll keep

G♭
D♭
trust - ing in Him un - til I see His
G♭
D♭/A♭
A♭7
4fr.
face. For He is my an - chor of
D♭
C♭/E♭
D♭7/F
G♭
D♭/A♭
hope. Yes, Je - sus is my
A♭7
4fr.
D♭
an - chor of hope.

Heaven's Hero

(featuring Champion of Love)

Words and Music by
PHIL CROSS

Majestic ♩ = 64

B♭/D C/E F B♭ C
7
moved a roy - al di - a-dem to re-ceive a crown of thorns, ex -
He paid the one price for a debt I could not pay.
B♭/D C/E F/A B♭
9
changed the prais - es of an - gels for the mock - er - y of men.
He's the one in the pre - sent, the end - ing and the start, the
Gm7 Edim7 Dm B♭ C/E F F/A
11
This is Heav - en's He - ro, my Sav - ior, Lord and Friend.
one, the on - ly he - ro is the He - ro of my heart.
Heav - en's
B♭ F/A B♭ Csus4 C/B♭ F/A B♭ C
14
He - ro I will fol - low; He is the Cap - tain of the

F F/A B♭ F/A B♭ C sus4 C/B♭
17
free. He will cham - pion my to - mor - row. Heav - en's
F/A B♭ C 1. F F/A C sus4/E B♭/D G m 3fr. D m/F C/E
20
He - ro is all I'll ev - er need.
2. F F/A B♭ F/A B♭ D m
23
need. He will cham - pion my to - mor - row. Heav - en's
F/C B♭/C C7 D♭/C♭ B♭m7 A♭m7 4fr. D♭/F
27
He - ro is all I'll ev - er need. He is

Champion of Love (Phil Cross, Carolyn Cross-English) *

G/D C♯m7(♭5) 4fr. D13 G/B
all - time un - dis - put - ed, un - de - feat - ed cham - pi - on. He will
C G/B C Em G/D
cham - pion my to - mor - row. Heav - en's He - ro,
G/B C Em G/D G/B Am7 G/A Dsus4 D D7sus4
Heav - en's He - ro, Heav - en's He - ro is all I'll ev - er
G G/B G/F♯ C/E Am7 G/A D7sus4 G/D G
need. He's all I need.
8vb

If It Takes a Valley

Words and Music by
JOEL LINDSEY and SUE C. SMITH

A E D
7
of pain.
Your will?
Yet, how
Have I
A E D
9
man - y saints I know a - bout have served You with - out an - y earth -
told You how it feels to face the en - e - my and know You're great - er
A E D
11
ly gain?
still?
In their
Yes, I
Bm D/A E/G#
13
suf - f'ring they dis - cov - ered Your suf - fi - cien - cy.
had to walk through dan - ger, Lord, so You could show
May - be
the way You

Bm
D/A
E
15
sac - ri - fice ___ is where ___ Your sweet - est
cov - er me ___ with mer - cy, and ___ You
bless - ings wait ___ for me. ___
nev - er let ___ me go. ___
D
A
E
17
___ If it takes ___ a val - ley to real - ly know ___ Your grace,
D
A
E
19
___ or if it's in ___ the des - ert where I'll meet You face ___ to face,
D
A
E
21
___ then turn the path ___ I'm trav - 'ling to some dark and lone - ly place. ___

F♯m
D
23
'Cause if it takes a val - ley,
A
25
then a val - ley's what I'll take.
G
D
1. A
27
G
D
E
2. D
A/C♯
29
2. Have I
I'm not say - ing cir - cum - stanc - es

D
D
32
nev - er cause me fear.
I'm just be - liev - ing
A/C♯
G
35
there is a pur - pose,
e - ven when it is - n't clear.
A
E
37
'Cause if it takes a val - ley
to real - ly know Your grace,
D
A
E
39
or if it's in the des - ert
where I'll meet You face to face...

D
F♯9sus4
B
F♯
41
If it takes a val - ley to real - ly know Your grace,
E
B
F♯
43
or if it's in the des - ert where I'll meet You face to face,
E
B
F♯
45
then turn the path I'm trav - 'ling to some dark and lone - ly place.
G♯m
4fr.
E
47
If it takes a val - ley,

B/D♯
50
if it takes a val - ley,
E
52
if it takes a val - ley,
then a val - ley's what I'll take.
B
54
A
E
B
56
A
E

I Have Not Forgotten

Words and Music by
RICKY ATKINSON and
LANCE CARPENTER

Gospel shuffle ♩ = 128

B
I must not for - get, with joy, not re - gret,
But in His ag - o - ny there was ran - som for me.
A
B
E
He died on the cross for all men.
His blood bought me joy with - out end.
E
Lord, I
A
E
E
have not for - got - ten Je - sus,

A
E
only begotten.
A
I was lost without hope
E
A
when the Lord saved my soul.
E
D♯dim
C♯m
4fr.
B
F♯m
B
I remember that hour, by His saving power, I

50
A
E
have not for - got - ten.
I
54
F♯m/A
E
2nd time to Coda
E
D♯dim
C♯m
4fr.
B
have not for - got - ten.
D.S. al Coda
59
F♯m
B
A
E
G♯m/B
4fr.
G♯m/C♯
4fr.
B/D♯
2. He was
CODA
64
E
D♯dim
C♯m
4fr.
B
F♯m
B
I'm washed in the blood,
His crim - son flood.
I

A
E
F♯m
E/G♯
69
have not for - got - ten.
I
A
E
73
have not for - got - ten.
E
D♯dim
C♯m
4fr.
B
F♯m
B
77
Ooo
Ooo
I
F♯m/A
E
81
have not for - got - ten.

I Will Trust You, Lord

Words and Music by
SHERYL FARRIS

Moderate two-feel 𝅗𝅥 = 76

D/A
B m
pass the pain right by.
But it just does - n't
e - ven crossed my mind.
But God's teach - ing me to
E
A
D
work that way. God has a dif - f'rent plan. He
trust Him more as He works His will in me. I
B m7
A
D
works in ways we'd nev - er see be - yond the scope of man.
rest se - cure - ly in His care, and sur - ren - der sure is sweet.
E sus4
E
A
When the jour - ney takes a de - tour

D
A
un - ex - pect-ed - ly, and I try to ac - cept and un - der -
D
Bm
stand what it all means, when I'm pressed to show the world
E7sus4
E7
what I real - ly be - lieve, I will
D
E/D
D
trust You, Lord.

E9sus4
A
When my heart be - gins to faint be - cause I
D
A
see a life so frayed, and my soul cries out, "O
D
Lord, how long can I keep this at bay?" In the
Bm
E7sus4
fierc - est part of bat - tle when my feet don't want to

E7
D
53
stay, I will trust You, Lord.
E/D
D
D
56
I will trust You, Lord,
E/D
D
E9sus4
A
60
with my life.
D
1.
2. D
A
64
2. I

Hey, Jonah

Words and Music by
DIANNE WILKINSON and SCOTT INMAN

B♭7
16
don't heed the Lord's com - mands. Don't take the wrong boat; it will
19
nev - er stay a - float, if the men did - n't throw you o - ver - board. Hey, Jo -
F7
B♭7
C7
22
- nah, don't you think it's a long way to sink? Don't you think you ought to lis - ten to the
F7
F7
25
Lord? 2. Jo - nah was a reb - el, he lis - tened to the Dev - il, his

28
ship sailed out from the shore. The waves start - ed rock - in', the wind
31
start - ed knock - in'. He was fright - ened like he nev - er had be - fore. They threw
B♭7
34
him off the side, and a whale was swim - ming by, swal - lowed him and looked a - round for
F7
B♭7
37
more. Hey, Jo - nah, don't you think it's a long way to sink? Don't you

C7
F7
B♭7
No, Jo - nah would - n't go.
think you ought to lis - ten to the Lord?
So the
'Cause Jo -
Lord had to put him in a place where he could - n't get a - way.
F
F7
- nah did - n't know.
When the Lord calls you forth you need to pack and leave that ver - y
B♭7
But God de - liv - ered he.
day.
So the whale gave him up, and his

52
F7
life and his call - ing were re - stored. Oh, Jo - nah learned the hard way, You
55
B♭7
C7
2nd time to Coda
bet - ter do the right thing. Jo - nah learned you ought to lis - ten to the
58
F7
Lord.
61
F7
3. The mor - al of the sto - ry: God got the glo - ry when the

64
Nin - e - vites re - pent - ed of their ways. Jo - nah fin - 'lly went there, he
67
set a lit - tle tent there, He preached and there were thou - sands who were saved. There's a mes -
B♭7
70
- sage here for all who will hear the Mas - ter's call, and do what Jo - nah just ig -
F7
B♭7
73
nored: Don't wait to learn the hard way. If Jo - nah could he would say,

C7
F7
D.S. al Coda
76
"You know you ought to lis - ten to the Lord." No, Jo -
CODA
F7
C7
79
Lord. Jo - nah learned you ought to lis - ten to the
F7
C7
82
Lord. Jo - nah learned you ought to lis - ten to the
F7
86
Lord!

Once Upon a Cross

Words and Music by
GINA BOE and MARTY FUNDERBURK

Dsus4 D Dsus4 D D/F♯
11
Rul - er of the u - ni - verse, God and God a - lone. But His
E/G♯ D/F♯ A/E D
13
heart was bro - ken by a world held cap - tive in their sin.
Bm Dm/F Dm6 E
15
A ran - som must be paid to re - deem them back to Him. So
Asus4 A Asus4 A Dsus4 D
17
God, in His great wis - dom, re - vealed His mas - ter plan: He'd send the Son of God to be -

D sus4 D D/F♯ E/G♯ D/F♯ A/E D
20
come the Son of Man. Once and for all the sac - ri - fice for sin would fi - n'lly be
B m A/C♯ D B 7/D♯ E sus4 E
23
Christ the per - fect Lamb up - on the cross of Cal - va - ry. One
A sus4 A A sus4 A D sus4 D
26
sin - gle act of match - less grace brought hope to all man - kind. One
A sus4 A F♯m7 G E sus4
28
drop of sin - less blood e - rased our guilt for all of time. One

D Dm/F A/E D A/C♯
30
mon - u - ment of mer - cy stands pro - claim - ing to the lost: The
Bm7 A/C♯ F♯m7 Bm7 A/C♯ Esus4 E
33
way was made, the price was paid once up - on a cross.
F/A G/A Asus4 A
36
Once the world could on - ly wait for the prom - ise held by faith. And
F/A G/A Asus4 A
38
once in low - ly Beth - le - hem, Mes - si - ah came to live with men. And

D m7
D m/C
B m7(♭5)
E7
A sus4
A m/G
40
once up-on Gol - go-tha's hill He bowed be-neath His Fa - ther's will to
F♯m7(♭5)
F7
E sus4
42
sat - is-fy re - demp-tion's cost, once up-on a cross.
F sus4
F
B♭sus4
B♭
B♭sus4
B♭
45
One sin - gle act of match - less grace brought
E♭sus4
E♭
B♭sus4
B♭
G m7
47
hope to all man - kind. One drop of sin - less blood e-rased our

A♭ 4fr.
F sus4
E♭
E♭m/G♭
49
guilt for all of time. One mon - u - ment of mer - cy stands, pro -
B♭/F
E♭
B♭/D
C m7 3fr.
B♭/D
G m7
51
claim - ing to the lost: The way was made, the price was paid
C m7 3fr.
B♭/D
F sus4
F
E♭/G
F/A
B♭
C m7 3fr.
B♭/D
G m7
54
once up - on a cross. The way was made, the price was paid
C m7 3fr.
B♭/D
F sus4
B♭
57
once up - on a cross!

Midnight Cry

Words and Music by
CHUCK DAY and GREG DAY

Moderately ♩ = 74

8
A♭
4fr.
D♭/A♭
And it's clos - er now___ than it's ev -
Oh, and signs of the times,___ they're ap - pear - ing ev -
11
E♭7sus4
E♭7
A♭
4fr.
A♭/C
4fr.
- er been.___ I can al - most hear the trum - pet___
- 'ry - where.___ I can al - most hear my Fa - ther___
14
D♭
A♭
4fr.
C7/G
Fm
D♭m/F♭
4fr.
___ as Ga - briel sounds the call.___ And at the
___ as He says, "Son, go get My chil - dren." And at the
17
A♭/E♭
4fr.
E♭7sus4
mid - night cry,___ we'll be go - in'___
mid - night cry,___ the bride of Christ will___

A♭ D♭ A♭ E♭9sus4 A♭ A♭/C
home.
rise.
When Je - sus steps out
D♭ A♭
on a cloud to call God's chil - dren,
C m7 F m B♭7
the dead in Christ shall rise to meet Him in the
E♭9sus4 E♭ A♭
air. And then those that re - main

D♭
A♭
C7
Fm
D♭m/F♭
4fr.
30
will be quick-ly changed.
At the
A♭/E♭
E♭9sus4
E♭
1.
A♭
D♭/A♭
11fr.
33
mid-night cry
when Je-sus comes
a - gain.
E♭/A♭
D♭/A♭
A♭
D♭/A♭
E♭/A♭
D♭/A♭
36
2.
A♭
E9sus4
39
a - gain.
And then those that re -

A D A C♯7/G♯
41
main will be quick - ly changed.
F♯m Dm/F A/E E9sus4
44
At the mid - night cry when Je - sus comes a -
A E9sus4 A/E
47
gain. Oh, at the mid - night cry
E9sus4 A D/A E/A E9sus4 A
50
when Je - sus comes a - gain, when Je - sus comes a - gain.